THE G
INVESTING

How to Bet NFL Football and Win

Written by Gregory Capello

Publication of OnlineWagerReview.com

Publication of www.onlinewagerreview.com

To my little Greggy,

One day you will be a big boy and be able to read this. And on that day, I hope you're proud of your Daddy.

Love, Dad

Acknowledgements

I wish to thank the following people for giving me the knowledge and support which allowed me to write The Guide to NFL Handicapping.

First, thank you to my beautiful wife Kristin. You have supported me in every set of our lives together. No matter what life has thrown us you have always stood by me. I love you.

Thank you Mom for always reassuring me I can do whatever I want in life if I put my mind to it. Thank you for your never ending love, encouragement and inspiration. I don't know where I would be in life with you. I love you Mom.

And thank you Dad, for teaching me about life, passion and hard work. You taught me everything I know about sports and Wall Street. This book (and most things in my life) would have never been possible without you.

Thank you to my Uncle John who has always been there to help guide me through life. Your inspiration and encouragement resonates deeper than you'll ever know.

And lastly, I would like to thank my entire family. You have always showing me the love that has helped me reach where I am today. No matter what happens in life, I God has blessed me with an incredible family.

TABLE OF CONTENTS

Introduction

As Labor Day draws closer each year, one of the biggest businesses in the World gets ready to restart. This seasonal business only operates for five months of the year, but generates billions of dollars in revenue. What is this business?

NFL Football Wagering.

In North America, Professional Football wagering is the king of sports betting. Experts estimate over $100 Billion is wagered on NFL football each season. To put this in perspective - if NFL football wagering was a country - its GDP would be ranked 60th in the World, just behind New Zealand.

A number of factors have caused the explosion of NFL betting popularity.

NFL Football receives incredible television coverage. News outlets, such as ESPN, Fox Sports and NFL Network analyze and break down every play of every game. With NFL Sunday ticket, an NFL fan can now watch all 16 games each week. Or, they can just watch every touchdown and scoring play on the NFL Networks "Red Zone Channel".

In addition to media coverage, the explosive growth of fantasy football has drawn fans even closer to the NFL action. Every year, the fantasy football participant spends countless hours researching teams, players and statistics. They risk money to enter their fantasy football league, which reduces the negative stigma towards "wagering" on football games.

Now packed with game analysis, football knowledge and player statistics - the NFL fan feels like an expert at the game. They risk money on their fantasy football teams and they are watching the games every week, so why not place a few wagers?

The NFL fan is now ready to take the leap into NFL wagering. They are ready to challenge the sportsbooks (and their wallets!) and place money on the point spread of the upcoming NFL games.

Why Did We Write The NFL Investing Guide?

Since our launch in 2006, Onlinewagerreview.com has providing our uses online sportsbook reviews, betting guides and free sports betting picks.

In our 6 years of operation, we have noticed a lack of solid NFL betting guides available to the aspiring NFL bettors. We found NFL founds eager to learn the arts of handicappers, but little material to support this thirst for knowledge.

In our view, the sports betting industry has failed to keep up with the desire for sports betting and handicapping knowledge. We decided to fill that void.

About Me

Before launching OnlineWagerReview.com, I spent 10 years as a trader on Wall Street. I made my living in stock speculation, trading and investments. As with many traders, my speculation did not end with stocks. I spend a large portion of my time developing a proprietary NFL investing system which combined statistical and emotional analysis. As my passion for sports betting grew, I saw a tremendous need for quality handicapping guides and sports betting information. So, this guide was born.

My approach towards sports betting is a simple one. I do not confuse myself with statistics and common belief. I approach NFL wagering with same investment type mentality as Wall Street money manager would approach stock speculation.

On Wall Street, it's important to understand the sentiment of the masses. Successful stock speculators properly gauge market sentiment to find "value" in stock price. When a stock price shows value because of the misconceptions of the investment public – they invest. As you will see, these are the same theories I bring to my NFL wagering strategy.

Now, after over 10 years of successful handicapping, I have decided to publish this guide. Through this guide, I will hope to teach you how to correctly view NFL wagering. How to properly gauge the sentiment of the betting public and sportsbook oddmakers. Furthermore, how to use this new found knowledge to your monetary advantage. Through our NFL investing process, we will find "value" in NFL betting lines and invest with success.

Where to Bet NFL Football

The Advantages of Online NFL Sportsbooks

With the explosive growth of NFL wagering - where are all the wagers being placed? Online and offshore sportsbooks have been the primary beneficiary of this betting surge. The legality of offshore wagers sometimes comes into question. But there has recently been a dramatic shift in sentiment towards online wagering. Cash strapped US states are looking for new ways to create tax revenue dollars. The legality of online betting could quickly be changing.

As we write this guide, the states of New Jersey, Delaware and California are making a strong push to legalize all online sports betting. With the negative sports betting bias fading, the American public is embracing the world of online sports betting.

Let's list the major advantages of wagering with an online sportsbooks:

- Ease of Use – ability to wager from the comfort of your home

- Take advantage of bonuses, promotions, loyalty programs and free bets

- Easily shop the best NFL lines and odds

- Payouts are never denied. They won't call you every 5 minutes when you owe money and they will not avoid you when it's time for a payout, like your local bookie will

- Lines offered early, many offshore sportsbooks have NFL lines available Sunday night. This will come in handy

- High betting limits - the top online sportsbooks have $50,000 maximum NFL wagers accepted.

It is important to understand - not all sportsbooks are created equal. OnlineWagerReview.com provides clients the top online sportsbooks, which can be fully trusted to accept your wagers and pay you on time. Our sportsbook review staff (and myself) have fully tested all online sportsbooks recommended by OWR. We use these sportsbooks ourselves!

Top NFL Sportsbooks Summary

The world of online sports betting can sometimes be confusing for newcomers. We often get asked what to expect when betting football online.

To make this process as simple as possible, we have outlined the online sportsbook signup for our users.

Visit www.onlinewagerreview.com/sportsbook-signup-guide for assistance with the sportsbooks signup, deposit and wagering process.

Regarding online sportsbook quality control, OnlineWagerReview.com does a great job of reviewing all top only sportsbooks. They are sure the sportsbooks they review are the best of the Internet. Only the sportsbooks that have a 100% track record of payouts, player security and excellent customer service make their review lists.

For more info on OWR's sportsbooks reviews – visit www.onlinewagerreview.com/sportsbook-reviews

NFL Betting Basics

Learn the Fundamentals of Football Wagering

In this chapter, we will review the basics of NFL betting. If you're a novice NFL bettor or would like a refresher in the fundamentals of NFL wagering, read through this section to understand the basics of how to wager on NFL football.

We will review types of NFL wagers, understanding football point spreads and how to read a sportsbook NFL listing. In addition to this section of the guide, we will list all the related NFL betting terms in the appendix section.

Note - If you are experienced in NFL wager, feel free to skip ahead to Part 3.

Point Spreads or Lines

Unlike other major sports, where a wager is placed on the outright winner of the game, betting on football involves a "point spread". A point spread is a handicap given to the perceived "favorite", in terms of points. For a favorite to win a point spread wager, they will not only have to win the game, but they will have to "cover the point spread".

On the flip side, an underdog can lose the game but still win a point spread wager. If an underdog losses (the game) by less points than the point spread is giving them, the underdog wins the wager.

Let's look at an example of an NFL point spread so we understand it clearly.

In this example, we will say New England Patriots are playing the New York Giants. For this matchup, it has determined the Patriots are a "7 point favorite". Conversely, the New York Giants have been set as a "7 point underdog". This is how this line, or point spread, would appear in a sportsbook:

Teams	Point Spread
New England Patriots	-7
New York Giants	+7

As you see in Table 2-A, for this Patriots/Giant point spread, there are 4 possible outcomes:

Table 2-A - Possible Outcomes	
Possible Outcomes	**Wager Winner**
Patriots win/Giants lose by 8 or more	Patriots
Patriots win/Giants lose by 7 points	Push or Tie
Patriots win/Giants lose by 1 to 6 points	Giants Win
Giants win/Patriots lose the game	Giants Win

The summary of the chart above is as follows – For the Patriots (favorite) to win the wager, they will need to "cover the point spread" and beat the Giants by 8 points or more. The Giants (as an underdog) have two ways to win the wager - win the game outright or lose by fewer than 6 points.

Note - In point spread betting, the favorite has one way to win the wager and the underdog has two. You can see statistics are already favoring underdogs in point spread betting. We will cover this dynamic in more detail later in the guide.

Sportsbook Fees – Juice, Vigorish or Vig:

When accepting an NFL point spread wager, a sportsbook collects a fee referred to as "juice", "vigorish" or "vig" for short. The standard sportsbook fee is 10% of your investment (or wager) amount. Another way to say this – we invest in NFL football wagering at 11 to 10 odds.

Here is an example of how "juice" comes into play in wagering dollars. Let's say for example you want to profit $100 by wagering on the New England Patriots. When placing your Patriots wager, you will need to risk (or invest) $110 to profit $100 on that wager.

- If you win the wager: you profit $100.

- If you lose the wager: you lose $110

- Profit/Loss Difference: $10 or 10%

This $10 (or 10%) difference in profit and loss is known as "juice". This is the fee a sportsbook charges for accepting your wager. This is how sportsbook generate revenue and realize profitability.

NFL Betting Basics Summary

In this section, we have outlined the very basics of NFL wagering, point spreads and vigorish. There are many different types of NFL proportions available, but for the purpose of this guide we will only be focusing on the betting points spreads (and the fees associated).

In the next part of the guide, we will discuss the creation of NFL points spreads. It is imperative we learn the motivations behind the setting of the point spread (and exploiting inconsistences). An understanding of this process will allow us to profit from point spread wagering.

How the NFL Line is Set

Motivations Behind the NFL Point Spread

In this chapter, we will learn how the NFL line is set by oddsmakers. Understanding this process is a fundamental part of our NFL football investing strategy. Our betting strategy takes advantage of the inaccuracies and public misconceptions that will lead to "value" in NFL betting lines. Here, we will guide you through the line setting process and analyze the motivations behind the NFL point spread.

As we noted in Part two, a point spread is a handicap given to "favorite", in terms of points. Let's look at another example of a point spread. In this example we will dig deeper and analyze the motivations behind why the point spread was set at that figure.

In the 2012 Super Bowl, the New England Patriots were a 3.5 point favorite versus the New York Giants. The Patriots were giving the Giants 3.5 points (add to their final score) in the game. This meant that the New England Patriots had to beat the New York Giants by 4 points or more for Patriot bettors to collect.

Why did the oddsmakers set the line at Patriots -3.5 points? Did they feel like this would be the final score? No. Did the oddsmakers try to predict the outcome of the game? Nope. Do line makers have a crystal ball? Guess again.

The oddsmakers set the line as Patriots -3.5 because they believed the Patriots were the favorite - *in the eyes of the public.* (Important, keep this phrase in mind)

When setting NFL lines, oddsmakers have one goal and one goal only – set a line so *both teams receive an equal amount of betting action.*

Let's repeat that again, another way – the oddsmakers could care less what the outcome of the game is. They are only concerned with dividing the amount wagered equal between both teams.

And how do the oddsmakers do this? Very simply. NFL oddsmakers have their finger on the pulse of the betting public. Oddsmakers are completely in tune with the sentiment of football bettors. They can predict, with very high accuracy, how bettors will react to a specific line. They weigh the emotions of the open market (or betting public) to determine what points spread (or line) will draw equal action.

So, that leads us to our next question. Why do oddsmakers want to achieve equal betting action on an NFL game?

The reason - *sportsbooks incur no risk when there is equal betting action on an NFL game.*

Let's look at an example so we understand this further.

Using the 2012 Super Bowl example, oddsmakers set a 3.5 point line to draw equal action on the game. Using hypothetical figures, $1100 was bet on New England and $1100 was wagered on New York. In this wagering scenario, the sportsbook has no risk of losing money. Let's continue.

The Giants won the 2012 Super Bowl wager. The sportsbooks will payout $1000 to the Giants bettors. And collect $1100 from the New England losers. The sportsbooks nets a profit of $100. Or, the sportsbooks collected their 10% fee.

Let's say, for example, the line was set at New York Giants +7. This line would have mis-gauged the sentiment of the betting public. This would have led to heavy, one side betting action on the Giants. With one-sided betting action, the sportsbooks profits are at risk. Continuing the example, $2000 is now bet on the Giants +7 and $0 bet on the Patriots -7 points. If the Giants win this wager the sportsbooks will take a large hit.

As you can see, odds makers determine NFL "point spreads" with the sole purpose of equaling out betting action.

How the Point Spread is Created Summary

In summary, the sole purpose of the oddsmaker is to equal out betting action. The importance of understanding this logic cannot be stressed enough. The fact that NFL lines are set using "feel" towards the sentiment of the betting public leads to lines that can inaccurately reflect the outcomes of games. Discovering the value in these inaccurate lines is where we will be focusing our attention and investing our NFL wagering dollars.

In this guide, we will show you how to discover these inaccuracies and realize "value" in NFL betting lines. We will give you tools and knowledge necessary to uncover this value and profit from it.

NFL Investing Ground Rules

The Basic Rules and Mindset of an NFL Investor

Approaching football investing with the correct mindset is essential to a profitable and successful NFL betting strategy.

Before we get into the investing strategy, it's prudent we layout some general handicapping ground rules to follow. These basic ground rules are essential to any betting. Regardless your NFL investing approach, these rules are a common denominator among successful sports betting professionals.

Rule #1 - Always Lean Towards the Underdog

This is rule number one. Always lean towards taking the underdog. Underdogs will make you money. As you will read in this guide, our NFL investing system allows us to find value in underdogs and exploit inaccurate lines.

There is a little known fact in the professional handicapping world - *There are no long-term winning handicappers that do not bet mostly (or solely) on underdogs.*

This may be difficult to believe, but it's true. And here is another fact - *you* will not start winning consistently until you adopt this mantra. Why is this you may ask? Well, let us explain.

Reason #1) Underdogs give you two chances to win a wager – this is a statistical anomaly of point spread betting. All things aside, there are 3 possible outcomes to a point spread wager. The underdog wins 2/3 of these outcomes - covering the spread or winning the game outright.

Reason #2) The team leading in a game rarely tries to score points - Seldom do we see a team, who is leading late in the game, try to score more points. When leading late, most NFL teams move to "prevent mode". Prevent mode is when a team leading the game merely tries to hold on to their lead. If you bet on a favorite and they are not covering the spread with a few minutes remaining, your investment is in trouble.

On the contrary, the losing team is always trying to come back and score points. If an underdog is losing a game, they will continually try to move the football and put points on the scoreboard. Often, against a prevent defense, which will allow yardage to be gained.

Reason #3) It is always easier to find value in underdog lines. As you start to understand the motivations of oddsmakers, and the betting public, you will see that it is easier to identify value in underdogs than it is in favorites. For a variety of reasons, oddsmakers often over compensate for favorites. They know the betting public likes to bet favorites and they add points accordingly. In these overcompensations we will find inaccuracies. In these inaccuracies is where we find value. In this value is where we will invest our NFL betting dollars.

Rule #2 - Be Disciplined. Do Not Bet for the Sake of Betting

In the world of stocks speculation, it's a cardinal sin to make a trade 'just because'. A seasoned Wall Street investor would not dare make an investment without first doing his or her homework. We will take this same approach with our NFL wagering.

Do *not* place a wager without realizing true value in your NFL investment. In this guide we will show you a discipline approach to placing your NFL wagers and investment. Stick to your game plan. Placing a wager without the proper preparation is a losing proposition.

Rule #3 - Be Confident...but Not Cocky

As in any successful business the owner, president or CEO needs to display a certain confidence in himself and in the strategy of the business. We will bring the same positive mindset to our NFL wagering approach.

When investing in the NFL, we always display a confidence that believes in our system. This allows us to roll with the ebbs and flows of the season. Never be distracted or derailed by the unexpected.

Let's not confuse this with cockiness. We want you to remain confident enough to believe in your strategy, but humble enough to admit when you're wrong.

Rule #4 - Learn from Your Mistakes

You will have losses. They are inevitable. But, how we view losing investments, or wagers, makes the difference between a successful handicapper and a poor one.

Do not get discouraged by losses. Take every loss as a learning experience. Analyze how you handicapped the game. Recap your thought process involved. Try to determine how or what you could've done better and then apply it in the future. View losses as a positive learning experience that will make you a better handicapper, or investor, in the future.

Rule #5 - Treat NFL Betting Like a Business Venture

Going forward, handle your NFL investing like a business venture, or better yet – like a professional money manager.

Professional money managers are always prepared and are continually working at their craft. They do their homework. They are realistic with his wins and losses. They keep accurate records. They always apply proper money management technics. They get a feel of the overall sentiment of the market and use this knowledge to find value in their investments.

Approach NFL investing with the same type of work ethic, effort and attitude.

Investing Ground Rules Summary:

Following these basic rules outlined above will make you be more profitable sports investor from day one. No matter what betting

strategy you choose or whichever sport you decide to wager on -
these rules are universal to successful sports speculation and
investing.

Recapping the basic ground rules of NFL investing:

- Always, or mostly, bet underdogs
- Show discipline when wagering
- Be confident in your handicapping skills
- Learn from your mistakes
- Treat NFL investing like a business

Investment Observations
How the NFL Works, How This Will Help Us Win

In this section, we will overview three general league observations in which we apply to our overall NFL investment strategy. We like to outline these points before we get into our specific investment system because these league dynamics will support our overall theory - *oddsmakers set inaccurate lines due to public betting sentiment.* These fundamental league observations will help you grasp the overall investment concept.

The following will highlight several points of how the NFL is viewed by oddsmakers and the NFL betting public. We will also introduce "team motivation". Motivation is an intangible in the game of football and a powerful way to find value in NFL lines.

Emotion and Motivation of the NFL players:

NFL players are human. The majority of the time, they are motivated and driven to succeed. Sometimes, they are lazy and lose focus. The 16 game NFL schedule is grueling one. Even the most successful teams will have weeks of emotional letdown. Overall, a football team's emotional ups and downs can greatly affect the outcome of football games.

Professional football handicappers and investors understand that *handicapping the emotional edge of the games can be of higher importance than the statistical one.*

It is very common in NFL Football for a team to perform well for two or three weeks, then they let their guard down. The players may get complacent. They do not practice as hard. The coaches pay less attention to detail, and so on.

On the contrary, a lesser NFL team may be emotionally charged or "gearing up" to face the perceived stronger opponent. They may be coming off several disappointing losses, perhaps embarrassing ones. Now this team, who was written off by the betting public, is looking to bounce back. Then, to everyone's surprise, a more emotionally motivated football team, of lesser skill level, keeps a game close or possible wins the game outright.

When placing our NFL wagers, we will strongly consider these emotional highs and lows a team encounters. In Part 7, we will define several specific situations that present an emotional edge, often not perceived by the betting public and certainly not factored into the betting line. Remember – when an emotional edge is present, it could outweigh skill level and ultimately determine the outcome of the game and your investment.

NFL Football is a Game of Parity

There is tremendous parity in the NFL. From season to season, the changes in the league standings are drastic and often unpredicted.

Unlike college football, at the NFL level there is only a small difference between the highest skilled player at each position and the least skilled. Because of this, the teams overall skill differential is separated by a very slim margin.

This margin of skill level is misperceived by the average NFL fan and bettor. This creates a "favorite oriented" type of betting sentiment. Oddsmakers know this fact well. Remember, oddsmakers set the lines according to the public sentiment. This favorite centric betting behavior forces oddsmakers to overcompensate and inaccurately set lines for favorites (giving the favorite too many points). Thus, *underdogs have greater investment value.*

Throughout our investment approach, we will look for these types of line inaccuracies and invest when the opportunities present themselves. The fact is - successful NFL investors make a living going against public sentiment and betting solely on underdogs.

Point Spread Nullifies Team Advantages:

Continuing the favorite centric view of novice NFL bettors, a common thought is widely accepted – the better team (or favorite) will "blow out" an inferior opponent and cover the spread, with ease. You will often here statement such as this – "I can't believe the Giants are only giving the Browns 7 points!?"

Is this common perception towards favorites the correct one? Let's look at some statistics to find out.

For this statistical study, we researched the NFL betting statistics for the 2011 season. We compared the combined records of favorites and underdogs. We looked at these records both straight up (outright winner) and against the point spread. Here are the results:

2012 NFL Football Betting Trends		
Straight Up or Outright Winner (SU)		
	Record	Percentage
Favorites	179-88	**67%**
Underdogs	88-179	33%
Against the Spread (ATS)		
Favorites	126-130-11	49%
Underdogs	*130-129-11*	*51%*

Explaining the findings above - when oddsmakers set a team as a favorite, the team won the game outright (or straight up) 67% (or 2/3rds) of the time. But, when we factor in the point spread - the favorite only won 49% of the games. *The underdog covered 51% of games when involving the point spread.*

Thus, when we take the point spread into consideration, the *underdog is the statistical favorite.*

From these statistics we can deduce - a point spread (set by oddsmakers) nullifies any skill advantage a favorite has over an inferior opponent.

Another way to say this - a point spreads puts the two opposing teams on a level playing, regardless of skill level. From this we can conclude - bettors who invest in favorites are often investing in poor value.

This is more ammunition reinforcing our overall NFL investment view. As the statistics show, betting the underdog is a statistical favorite and will show you good investing value. We foresee no change in these NFL betting trends. Underdogs will continually show NFL investors the most value for our NFL betting dollars.

Observations of NFL Football Summary

In summary, the observations above provide us confirmation for our overall NFL investment approach. First, we have learned that the emotional edge in NFL football is a powerful one, is often outweighing skill level. Next, we discussed how NFL parity has caused very slim margins between position skill levels, which are misconceived by the betting public. Finally, we showed how underdogs are statistical favorites when point spreads are involved. A point spread nullifies any skill level advantage.

Recap of NFL observations:

- Emotions - Emotions affect the outcomes of games. Understanding and handicapping emotions is an important part of a finding value and winning NFL investing

- NFL Parity - there is great parity in NFL Football. The skill margin between teams is very small. Often smaller than the public perceives. This causes underdogs to have value.

- Point Spreads – lines set by oddsmakers nullify any advantage a more skillful team has. Betting favorites often has poor value. Focus on betting underdogs.

NFL Power Rankings

The Key to Finding NFL Investment Value

With the foundational mindset laid out in previous chapters, we will now get to the core of our NFL investment strategy. Our NFL handicapping investment strategy is based on NFL team "Power Rankings".

Power rankings defined – *a letter grade, set on each team, that tells where that club stands in skill and strength, in relation with the rest of the league.*

In its simplest form, we use power rankings to determine the difference between two teams, predicting what the point differential in the game will be. The predicted outcomes will allow us identify inaccurate NFL lines. Hence, find NFL investing value.

When we are learning the basics of our power ranking system we will hold some variables constant 1) All players are healthy 2) the game is played on a neutral field and 3) emotional edges do not exist. Of course these constants do not hold true in a real world setting, but later we will make adjustments for these variables, accordingly.

As you will see, the use of power rankings will allow us too statistically (and unemotionally) isolate the value realized when NFL lines are set inaccurately.

How we set Power Rankings:

First, we will learn how to set our proprietary NFL handicapping power rankings. This is a simple process that removes the unnecessary noise when handicapping an NFL team or matchup.

When setting your team ranking (or letter grade) we use two determining factors 1) how is a team currently playing and 2) what will the team's record be after a full 16 game schedule.

Taking these factors into account, we create our power rankings by applying a specific letter grade to all 32 teams in the NFL. Refer to Table 7-A for the power ranking letter grade chart.

Table 7-A Overall Record Power Rankings		
Grade	Overall Wins	Overall Losses
A	16	0
A	15	1
A	14	2
A	13	3
B+	12	4
B	11	5
B-	10	6
C+	9	7
C	8	8
C-	7	9
C-	6	10
D+	5	11
D	4	12
D-	3	13
F	2	14
F	1	15
F	0	16

How to Use the Power Rankings Chart (Table 7-A)

If we analyze an NFL football team and after reviewing their overall play we conclude that team is playing as an overall 8 win team (8-8 record overall) we then apply a 'C' ranking on that team. As you can see, C grade (as it implies) is the median grade, an average NFL team.

On the top of the scale, you find the letter grade of 'A'. The A graded teams are (as the grade implies) the class of the league. An example of a team with an A grade would be the 2011 Green Bay Packers. During the 2011 season, Green Bay continually showed throughout the season they were able to cover spread, put up points and play solid defense (among other things). All A graded teams should show characteristics of a Super Bowl contending team.

On the bottom grading scale, we have worst teams in the league. Grade D- through F would define an inferior classed NFL team. An example of the lowest grade possible would be the 2009 St. Louis Rams. These lowest graded teams are characterized by lack of ball movement, do not protect the football and ultimately do not prevent teams from asserting their game plan.

It's worth noting at this time that the majority of NFL teams fall between B+ (12-4) and D+ (5-11) record. In this grade area where most of our handicapping will take place. This grade range is where we will be able to find the most investment value.

Determining Power Rankings:

Setting your NFL team power rankings is not an exact science. This is where you're NFL handicapping and investment knowledge will come into play. Just as in stock or real estate speculation, opinions towards investments are subjective. And this is what creates the beautiful open market, we call capitalism, but that's a conversation for another time!

Bottom line is - Determining your power rankings is where handicapping, investing skill, a proper mindset, hard work and experience (all rolled into one!) comes into play.

Additional note on power rankings - throughout the NFL season, OWR provides proprietary weekly NFL power rankings. These rankings are determined with over 25 years of NFL betting experience and proprietary knowledge of the investing system. For more information on OWR's proprietary power rankings visit www.onlinewagerreview.com/nfl-rankings

If you would like to set your own proprietary rankings, you are more than welcome. That is one of the beauties of the investing system. You can set your own letter grades based on your subjective view of the NFL. To set your own rankings use the following questions as a guide:

- How is the team currently playing?
- What will this team's record be at the end of the season?
- Are there any key injuries affecting the team's current outlook?

Injuries – How they Affect Power Rankings

Let's now review how to handle injuries. Again, this is subjective. We will ask ourselves during the grade setting process - *Are there any key injuries affecting the team's current outlook?*

Obviously, football injuries can vary greatly. A quarterback injury will have more effect on a team's play (and power ranking) then would an injured backup defensive lineman. So, make adjustments accordingly. Later, we will discuss when and how to research football injuries.

Weekly Adjustments to Your Power Rankings

It's important to note - power rankings are dynamic. Your team rankings are not a toaster. There's no "set it and forget it'" going on here. Your rankings will need to be updated religiously. This is part of our overall weekly routine that we will cover in Part 9.

When making weekly adjustments we will use a combination of the factors (outlined above). During the weekly updates we will include the most recent information acquired (last game played). And as you will see throughout the season, these dynamic power ranking adjustments we will continual find betting value, often overlooked by the betting public.

Average Margin of Victory vs. Overall Record, Correlated?

Before we get to next step in the process, let me first outline how we concluded our *margin of victory vs. total wins* study. This will allows us to understand the point spreads, between different overall records (and how our proprietary lines are set), before we start putting our rankings into practice.

When I started to seriously handicap NFL football, I asked myself a simple question – Does a correlation exist between an NFL team's margin of victory and that team's overall record?

Table 7-B Correlation Between Margin of Victory and Overall Record		
Ranking	Average Margin of Victory	Total Wins
A	10.5	13 to 16
B+	7.5	12
B	5.5	11
B-	4	10
C+	3	9
C	0	8
C-	-3	7,6
D+	-6	5
D	-7.5	4
D-	-9	3
F	-13	2 to 0

The Guide to NFL Investing

In other words, I wanted to see if there were any common patterns between a team's overall record (end of the season) and how many points they won or lost by. Well, I decided to conduct a statically study to try to figure it out. The results of the study were very surprising. Let's review the study and findings.

For the sake of time (and trees!), I will keep this in summary. To perform this study, I took data from the last 10 years (2001 to 2011) of NFL team stats and performed calculations on final records versus margin of victory. In Table 7-B, you will find the conclusions of this statistical study. You will see the correlation between average margin of victory and a team's overall record.

Note – Because of statistical anomalies (such as the 16-0 Patriots) the results have been slightly tweaked. For the raw data of this study, see the appendix section.

As you can see, there's clearly a correlation between a team's overall record and their average margin of victory. The higher the number of wins translates into higher margin of victory (and vice versa). Furthermore, the margins of victory statistics (versus overall record) fall into consistent intervals.

This was the missing piece in my NFL investing system. Now, armed with these cold, hard statistics we are able to apply them to our rankings and *set our own lines*.

Home Field Advantage – How Do We Factor?

One quick note on home field advantage – how do we compensate for it?

In our system, the standard *home field advantage is worth -2.5 points*, in favor of the home team. Another words, we will be deducting 2.5 points from our margin of victory number (as you will see later).

There are some exceptions to this rule (the 12th Man in Seattle, the silent crowd of the lonely Jaguars or the frozen tundra of Lambeau Field). These exceptions will be subjective based on specific circumstances. OWR makes these adjustments in our proprietary picks and rankings and you are free to do the same.

To keep it simple, we will be using this standard home field advantage (of -2.5 points) going forward in this guide.

Let's Play Oddsmaker. Setting your Own NFL Line

Knowledge of point spread creation? Check. Letter grades defined? Check. Record vs. margin of victory determined? Done. Now, it's time to piece it all together.

The simplest way to explain this step in the process is – *we become the oddsmaker.* We will use our team's power rankings and apply them to an NFL matchup. Through the ranking differences we will be able to determine our own proprietary football point spread.
In essence - we set *our* point spread.

So, how do we do this? How do we use power rankings to become an oddsmaker? Let's explain.

For this step, will be reviewing a specific game. For each team playing in this particular game, we take our predetermined power rankings (placed on those two teams) and calculate the difference (point margin differential) between opposing letter grades.

To understand this process, let's look at some specific examples of setting our own lines.

Example #1 - Miami Dolphins (C) at New York Jets (B+)

For this example, we have graded the Miami Dolphins as C team. As we noted above, we have taken into consideration all the variables of power rankings and have determined the Dolphins are currently an 8-8 football team. We have done the same for the New York Jets and we have determined them to be a 12-4 football team, hence the B+ grade.

By using the Table 7-2 we can infer the following:

- Miami Dolphins (C) average margin of victory is 0 points.

- New York Jets (B+) average margin of victory is 7.5 points

With this information we can now set our own line for the Dolphins vs. Jets game. The difference between the Miami Dolphins and New York Jets is 7.5 points. Let's set our first line using our power rankings and margin of victory:

Team	Grade	Point Spread
Miami Dolphins	C	+7.5
New York Jets	B+	-7.5

But wait. We are not done yet. We have to compensate for home field advantage. In this example - The New York Jets are the home team, so we will deduct 2.5 points (standard home field advantage) from their point spread. After doing that we have a final line that looks like this:

Team	Grade	Point Spread
Miami Dolphins	C	+10
New York Jets	B+	-10

Compare Your Lines to Sportsbook (Oddsmaker) Betting Lines

Now that we have set our proprietary line for the Miami Dolphins at New York Jets game - it's time to compare it to the sportsbook (or oddsmakers) point spread. With a few clicks of the mouse we reach our top online sportsbook and find the Dolphin at Jets game listed as follows:

Team	Point Spread
Miami Dolphins	+13
New York Jets	-13

When we compare the line above with *our line* - do we see value? We absolutely do.

As we have learned, oddsmakers have set their lines (like the one above) by gauging the sentiment of the betting public. In this case, the odds makers have inaccurately set the New York Jets as favorite *3 points greater than what we have calculated*. There could be several reasons for this, but regardless - we have discovered NFL betting value. These are lines we will invest in going forward.

Let's practice more examples.

Example #2 - Philadelphia Eagles (B-) at Dallas Cowboys (C-)

For this example, we are handicapping the Philadelphia Eagles at the Dallas Cowboys. Through our weekly power ranking adjustments and by weighing all variables we have determined the Eagles to be a B- team (10-6 record) and the Cowboys to be a C-team (7-9 record).

Let's now set *our* line, but instead of calculating by hand, this time we will use our "Power Rankings/Point Spread Cheat Sheet". (Before introducing the cheat sheet we wanted to be sure you understood the basic concept.)

You will find the Power Rankings/Point Spread Cheat Sheet in Table 7-3. You will also find a copy in the appendix section.

How to Read the Power Rankings/Point Spread Cheat Sheet

The home team power ranking grade is found on the top chart (columns). On the left side of the chart you will find the away team's power ranking grade (rows). Find the letter grades you have set on the teams in a specific game and where the home team (column) meets the away team (row) is where you will find your line for the *home team.*

To figure the away team's point spread, just flip the number (from negative to positive or vice versa).

Note - the standard home field advantage (of -2.5) has already been calculated in this table.

Table 7-C
Power Rankings/Point Spread Cheat Sheet

	Home Team										
	A	B+	B	B-	C+	C	C-	D+	D	D-	F
A	-2.5	0.5	2.5	4	5	8	11	14	15.5	17	21
B+	-5.5	-2.5	-0.5	1	2	5	8	11	12.5	14	18
B	-7.5	-4.5	-2.5	-1	0	3	6	9	10.5	12	16
B-	-9	-6	-4	-2.5	-1.5	1.5	4.5	7.5	9	10.5	14.5
C+	-10	-7	-5	-3.5	-2.5	0.5	3.5	6.5	8	9.5	13.5
C	-13	-10	-8	-6.5	-5.5	-2.5	0.5	3.5	5	6.5	10.5
C-	-16	-13	-11	-9.5	-8.5	-5.5	-2.5	0.5	2	3.5	7.5
D+	-19	-16	-14	-12.5	-11.5	-8.5	-5.5	-2.5	-1	0.5	4.5
D	-20.5	-17.5	-15.5	-14	-13	-10	-7	-4	-2.5	-1	3
D-	-22	-19	-17	-15.5	-14.5	-11.5	-8.5	-5.5	-4	-2.5	1.5
F	-26	-23	-21	-19.5	-18.5	-15.5	-12.5	-9.5	-8	-6.5	-2.5

Away Team (left vertical label)

Now that we have the cheat sheet tool available, let's continue with the Eagles at Cowboys example. Recapping, the Eagles are a B- team on the road versus a Cowboys team we rank as a C-.

Let's use our cheat sheet in Table 7-C to determine our line for the game. We find Cowboys C- in the home team columns

The Guide to N(F...)

(along the top) of the chart and then we follow it down to the Eagles B- grade row. Home field advantage is already calculated in, so we are ready to set our line:

Team	Grade	Point Spread
Philadelphia Eagles	B-	-4.5
Dallas Cowboys	C-	+4.5

Now, the next step in the process is to compare our line to the sportsbook/oddsmaker line. We navigate to our online sportsbook and discover the Eagles at Cowboys line is as follows:

Team	Point Spread
Philadelphia Eagles	-7.5
Dallas Cowboys	+7.5

Do we see investing value in the sportsbook line above? You bet we do. (No pun intended).

Again, we have used our power rankings and margin of victory statistics to identify another inaccurate line. Multiple factors may be leading to the oddsmaker's overcompensation on the Eagles as a favorite. But, as far as we are concerned, the betting public has given too much credit to the Eagles in this match up. The oddsmakers have made the line adjustment to compensate for the public sentiment. We have discovered it. And now we will invest in the Cowboys +7.5 points.

Let's review one more scenario, a slight variation from the first two examples.

Example #3 - New England Patriots (B+) at Buffalo Bills (D+)

For this example, we will handicap the match up of the New England Patriots traveling to the Buffalo Bills. Through our research and power ranking adjustments we have concluded the Patriots are a B+ team and the Bills are a D+ team.

Next, we will us our Power Rankings/Point Spread Cheat Sheet in Table 7-3 to play oddsmaker and determine our line. We calculate the following Patriots at Bills point spread:

Team	Grade	Point Spread
New England Patriots	B+	-11
Buffalo Bills	D+	+11

The next step, compare our line to the sportsbook/oddsmaker line. We find the oddsmakers have set Patriots at Bills point spread as:

Team	Point Spread
New England Patriots	-7.5
Buffalo Bills	+7.5

Do we see value in the line above? Do we now bet the Patriots because they have been *undercompensated* as a favorite versus the Bills? This is a trick question.

As we have learned, underdog betting is where we will place the majority of our NFL investment emphasis. Using our power rankings and margin of victory, we do see value in the Patriots -7.5, *but* with all things being equal, I would not bet the Patriots in this example.

In our investing system, we try to solely focus our attention (and investments) on underdogs. In this scenario, you are free to invest in the Patriots -7.5. But a word of caution – tread lightly with situations such as this.

I would advise you to be very selective in scenarios where you conclude value in betting a favorite. The reason is – we are focusing primarily on underdogs. Favorites sometimes offer a profitable proposition, but keep in mind you will have the favorite/underdog dynamics (highlighted in Part 5) working against you.

Power Rankings Summary:

Let's recap everything we have learned in this chapter:

- The use of NFL power rankings and margin of victory statistics will allow you discover NFL investing value

- Remember power rankings are not an exact science. It will take many hours of hard work to perfect and refine

- I will be providing my proprietary power rankings (and picks based off rankings) to premium users at OnlineWagerReview.com

Steps to setting your proprietary power rankings, playing oddsmaker and comparing your lines to the sportsbook/oddsmaker's lines:

- Set your power rankings (on all 32 teams) taking into consideration - current level of play, season end record and player injuries

- Adjust your rankings weekly using information from the past weeks games

- Set your own line for each weekly matchup - using the Power Rankings/Point Spread Cheat Sheet
- Compare your point spread to the sportsbook/oddsmakers line
- Invest in underdogs where you discover value

You have just learned my proprietary NFL investing system. This system been developed over 15 years, refined through testing and countless hours of statistical study. It has been provided in the hopes you too can gain financial from my NFL investing system.

But, we are not finished yet. In the next few chapters we will cover emotional edges, statistics to help you set power rankings, planning your betting week and money management.

In the next chapter we will uncover specific scenarios which provide a team with an emotional edge.

Emotional edges, combined with your new found power rankings, will have the bookies running for cover!

Emotional Edges

10 Specific Scenarios that Create an Emotional Edge and Investment Value

As we have learned - finding inaccurate lines, due to incorrect public betting sentiment, is at the heart of successful NFL value investing. Now, we will learn about the power the emotional edge in football.

We define an emotional edge as – an intangible force that causes a football team to have added motivation for an upcoming game or opponent.

Furthermore, an emotional edge allows a *team to play beyond their skill level*, which often goes unnoticed by the general betting public. Hence, emotional edges are not compensated for in the oddsmaker's line and investment value is realized.

In this chapter, we will highlight 10 specific NFL game scenarios which create an emotional edge. We will review these scenarios and analyze the reasons why a team will be more emotionally charged for an upcoming matchup or opponent.

Before we get into the 10 scenarios - I would like to make mention of "NFL Investing Quarters".

NFL investing quarters allow us to break the NFL calendar into different segments. During these different quarters, we will be making slight mental and investing adjustment. These adjustments will allow you to stay one step ahead of the sportsbooks, betting public and the ever changing sentiment throughout the season.

Note – With the following scenarios, we will continue to focus primarily on betting underdogs.

NFL Investing Quarters

Just as Wall Street views their calendar year, we break down the NFL calendar into 'investing quarters'. These quarters will be broken down as follows:

- NFL Q1: Week 1 through Week 4
- NFL Q2: Week 5 through Week 8
- NFL Q3: Week 9 through Week 12
- NFL Q4: Week 13 through Week 17

As we mentioned, in each NFL quarter, our investment strategy will change slightly. These small adjustments are made to stay ahead of the betting public and oddsmakers compensation towards sentiment shifts.

NFL Q1 - Week 1 through Week 4

In Weeks 1 through 4 - the betting public is primarily basing their league views and opinions on information from the *prior year*. In essence, oddsmakers set their lines based on information that is 12 months old, and widely incorrect. This is music to an NFL investors ears!

Because of this, we will find it easier to discover inaccurate lines and 'false favorites' during this time frame. False favorites are teams that should not be favored in the game, misconceptions have caused a grossly inaccurate line.

In this part of the season, we will be utilizing our power rankings to their fullest. With good individual team handicapping (and our Point Spread/Margin Tools) we will be able to discover inaccurate lines and excellent investing value.

Note – emotional edges are more difficult to find during this Quarter. The season is just underway and the dynamics that would cause an emotional edge are yet to come into play.

Additional note about NFL Q1 - In this first quarter we will *never* be laying points or betting on favorites. Lines are being set on incorrect information, the good teams have yet to be determined and most favorites prove to be wrong.

NFL Q2 - Week 5 through Week 8

In weeks 5 through 8, the class of the league is starting reveal itself. We will start to more accurately determine the more skillful teams from the inferior ones.

Our weekly power rankings will become more accurate. As more games are played, more information will become available. We will us this new found information to set our rankings and to form our overall opinion on the league.

During this Quarter, the betting publics overall outlook on the league may get better, too. But, regardless of their improvement, there will still be many incorrect perceptions towards individual teams and matchups. We still find plenty of opportunities to find imprecise lines and investing value.

In this segment, emotional edges start to take shape. Something we like to call "schedule analysis" will become an important part of identifying upcoming emotional edges. Later, we will learn about scheduling analysis and outline some specific scheduling scenarios which will create the intangible of a motivational edge.

NFL Q3 - Week 9 through Week 12

In Q3 of the NFL season we will continue to find inaccurate lines (using our Power Ranking Tools) and continue to focus on emotional edges that exist in specific scenarios. Emotional edges will start to carry more weight during this stretch of the season. Because the grueling NFL season may start to effect teams in a different way, understanding the mental mindset of the teams will play a larger part in finding inaccurate lines.

We will also be putting more emphasis on statistics during this portion of the season. But, not the meaningless statistics you will hear on television. Rather, statistics that uncover the true ability of an NFL football team.

So, why do we start to put more weight into stats? Simple - the information has become available. As Gordon Gecko once said – "The most valuable commodity I know of is information". Same holds true in NFL investing.

We will cover statistics in the next chapter, but this is a good time to point out – *do not confuse yourself with statistics*. Do not let stats come between you and finding good point spread value.

With all the mountains of NFL information available, statistical analysis can become confusing and cumbersome. Keep your statistical investment approach a simple one. Only use the stats that have high correlation to win rate (as we will show you). And only use them to make modifications to your Power Rankings.

NFL Q4 – Week 13 to Week 17

As the season winds down, understanding the mental mind set of every team will become impetrative. We continue to relying heavily on Power Rankings, margin of victory tools, and weekly adjustments. But, intangible forces, such as playoff position, playoff bye weeks, draft position, revenge games (more on this later) or players just wanting play golf could make an enormous impact on the outcomes of games.

Because of these factors, during Q4 you will have to be more in tune with the emotional side of football. Teams will be motivated by factors unseen by the untrained handicapping eye.

This could possibly the most difficult portion of the season to handicap. But don't be alarmed. Value will still be created. Misconceived public betting sentiment will still show us inaccurate lines. But the creation of value could come from unforeseen circumstances, often creating unique motivational edges - too numerous to outline in this investment guide.

10 Situations that Create an Emotional Edge

Now that we have covered the different NFL investment quarters we are ready to dive into the specific scenarios that create an emotional edge. Keep in mind, these scenarios don't act alone. When you combine - effective power rankings, weekly adjustments and the ability to identifying emotional edges - it will give you the ability to realized NFL investment value like never before.

#1) An Underdog Getting 4 points or more...

Basically, it's just another way to say - focus on underdogs. But now let's look at the emotions a team encounters when perceived as an underdog.

The fact is - NFL teams/players know when they're set as an underdog. And, they don't like it. This causes them to have a more spirited week of practice. They will prepare harder to face the upcoming 'better' opponent.

The betting public often underestimates (or ignores) this added motivation the underdog holds. Holding to their favorite bias mentality, the public will wager on this favorite, in the thoughts - the favorite will have no problem covering the spread.

Going forward, never overlook 'underdog motivation'. Being set as an underdog creates a motivation that goes unnoticed by the betting public. And of course, use your Power Rankings tools to determine if this underdog is showing you investment value.

#2) Home Underdogs, Especially in Home Opener

Home underdogs. Music to an NFL investors ears.

I cannot begin to tell you how much success I have had betting home underdogs. And, I am not alone. Many professional NFL handicappers make a living wagering *only* on home underdogs.

A home underdog scenario creates an enormous emotional edge for the home team.

There are several factors at play here. 1) The team knows they are a home underdog. 2) With the pride of NFL players, they will not allow a perceived better team to visit their home field and walk all over them. 3) In the words of Ray Lewis – "We must protect this house." This is the mantra of the NFL.

The here theory is simple one. The betting public perceives the road team to be a better team. The oddsmakers compensate for the sentiment (with no regard to the outcome of the game). The home team's pride sets in and they declare "there is no way we let this better team come in here and make us look foolish".

This is a great example of how an emotional edge is created. Furthermore, this produces excellent investment value for the bettors able to identify a situation such as this.

Additional note on Home underdogs - this scenario becomes even more powerful when it's a home underdogs *first home game of the year.*

The "home opener" is an inspiring scenario for NFL teams, creating an enormous emotional edge. In NFL Q1, put extra emphasis on underdogs in home openers.

#3) Team scores 35+ points two consecutive weeks, letdown coming

The betting public takes notice when a team starts to light up the scoreboard. The sentiment towards this high-powered offense will be "that team is unstoppable. No way do they not cover every spread for the rest of the season".

Who also takes notice of these high powered offenses and sentiment shift of the public? You guessed it – the oddsmakers.

Scoring 35+ points in two consecutive weeks will often lead to two things happening 1) the oddsmakers *overcompensate* for the sentiment shift of the betting public. 2) Possible complacency by the good offensive team the following week.

The opposing defensive unit will take notice, too. While sitting in weekly film study, they will put extra emphasis on shutting down this perceived offensive juggernaut. This will often lead to added determination and an emotional edge for the unit.

On one hand you have the oddsmakers compensating the favorite extra points. On the other you have a defense who is extra motivated to face a perceived greater opponent. Put this all together and you have a receipt for betting value.

Look to wager against a big favorite that has scored 35+ points two consecutive weeks. Contrary to the public's perception, it will be difficult for this team to cover the point spread the following week.

#4) Prime Time game winner - Bet against the next week

For the scenarios 4 through 7, we will analyze how 'Primetime' games effect a team emotional mindset and the sentiment of the betting public.

Primetime games are defined as a football game played in the Thursday, Sunday or Monday night time slots.

Because these games are being watched by millions of fans (not to mention the other 30 teams in the league) they can have a profound effect on a team's overall emotional state. Furthermore, the betting public (and media) will put more emphasis on these games when developing opinions about the league.

As we can predict, oddsmaker make point spread adjustments in accordance with these sentiment shifts and media over-hyping (more on this later) that surrounds primetime games. The majority of the time, oddsmakers overcompensate for the public's enhanced view of the winning primetime team. This will create inaccurate lines, which in turn creates point spread value.

Pay close attention to the prime time winners and their lines for the following week. Of course, use your Power Ranking tools. In many cases you will discover value betting against the previous prime time game winners.

#5) Primetime Home Underdogs

As we discussed in scenario #2 – being a home underdog creates a powerful emotional edge, for the home team.

Now, when we combined this with the added motivation of prime time game – you have possibly the most power combination for an emotional edge we can find.

For this particular scenario, we have an added dynamic - the home town crowd. When a home town crowd is aware a (perceived) better team is coming into their house - they will be sure to make it a hostile environment.   Picture yourself as a fan. The anticipation for this upcoming 'big game' has grown and grown all week long. By the time game time rolls around, your emotions will be boiling over. The crowd, as a whole, will be rocking come kick-off time.

Always remember a home underdog, in a primetime game, creates a tremendous emotional edge.   This edge (like most) goes undetected by the general NFL bettor and value can be realized when investing in the point spread.

#6) Routed in Primetime, Sunday or Monday Night Embarrassments

Continuing the emotional effects a primetime games - If a team is *routed* (or blown out) in a primetime game, then look for them to bounce back strong the next week.

Multiple reasons here – 1) No one likes being embarrassed on national TV and in front of their peers 2) There is a very strong chance the previously embarrassed team will practice hard the next week and focus on bouncing back strong 3) the betting public will witness this blowout and discount the losing team the following week and 4) the oddsmakers will overcompensate for this primetime blowout.

How the Schedule creates Emotional Edges (or lack of)

Understanding the NFL schedule is an important part of realizing value in NFL investing. Point spread value can be realized if an investor understands the different emotional edges gained by scheduling scenarios.

In scenarios 7 through 10, we will introduce *"scheduling analysis"*. We will review how scheduling analysis is a powerful tool in identifying upcoming emotional edges.

For more details on how NFL schedule is created see the appendix section.

In its simplest form, scheduling analysis is the act of reviewing a team's upcoming schedule in an attempt to identify an emotional edge, or lack thereof.

Let's take this one step further – it's a widely accepted view NFL teams become more motivated to face their divisional opponents. And this is for good reason. Divisional games are the biggest games on a team's schedule. If a team doesn't play their division well, they won't make the playoffs.

Now, we are left with non-divisional games - how do teams view these games? With such a large emphasis is place on divisional games, teams tend to lose focus and the emotional edge when facing a non-divisional opponent. Generally speaking, non-divisional games can lead to emotional letdowns.

This division versus non-division dynamic creates opportunities for the NFL investor. The emotional edges gained or lost due scheduling forces are rarely noticed by the novice bettor, hence are unadjusted in the point spread.

#7) Divisional Victory followed by Non-Divisional Game

Divisional victory followed by a non-divisional game is an important scenario to watch for when doing scheduling analysis. When a team achieves a divisional victory then faces a non-divisional opponent the following week, and is favored, look to bet on the underdog.

Here is an example of this scenario:

- In Week 2 of the NFL season - Dallas Cowboys beat division rival NY Giants
- In Week 3, the Cowboys travel to play the Cleveland Browns (out of division and conference)
- The line is set for the Cowboys -7.5 at Browns +7.5

In the example above, the Dallas Cowboys achieved victory over a divisional rival. Now, the Cowboys are traveling to play a (perceived) lesser skilled Browns team (we know the Browns are perceived inferior because of the +7.5 point spread). The Cowboys could grow complacent after their big divisional win. They could look at their upcoming Browns game with lesser importance and a possibly view the game as an 'easy win'.

This type of scenario leads to an emotional letdown by the Cowboys. The divisional victory then non-divisional scenarios can provide excellent investment opportunities.

Additional Note - Throughout the season, pay extra attention to underdogs in non-divisional games. The betting public can overlook the letdown possibilities of a favorite in a non-divisional game.

#8) The Divisional "Sandwich Game"

A Divisional Sandwich Game is when a team plays a divisional game, then a non-division (or non-conference) game, then a divisional game the third week.

This is a variation of scenario 7, with an added kicker. Not only is the team coming off a divisional win, but there is an added dynamic. The team's third game in the series is versus another divisional rival. This team could get caught 'looking ahead'.

Looking past non-divisional opponents can lead to an emotional letdown. In this scenario, we will be looking to sell short (or bet against) the team in the "sandwiched" non-divisional game.

#9) Big Game Ahead - 'Better' Team Gets Caught Looking Ahead

We define a 'Big Game' as a game against a divisional rival or versus a top 5 team in the league.

This scenario is another variation of 'looking ahead'. Teams often have emotional letdowns, and play below their skill level, when they look ahead at Big Games. If an NFL team does not focus on the opponent at hand a letdown is probable. This occurs often in the NFL.

When you notice a team has big game upcoming - look to wager on the team to be perceived as less skillful (underdog). The oddsmakers will not compensate for the emotional letdown possibility. These big game/look ahead scenarios have a history of showing good investment value.

#10) The Revenge Game

The Revenge Game is defined as - a team lost to a divisional opponent, now faces them for a second time, in the same season.

As you can imagine, revenge games can create a strong motivational edge for a team who lost the previous contest. Revenge games can provide another good opportunity to capitalize on a hidden emotional edge.

This is how we handle Revenge Games - In our experience, if two teams are close to Power Rankings (C- to B-) it will be difficult for a team to beat another twice in one season.

When handicapping a Revenge Game, view how the teams resulted in their first meeting. Do the oddsmakers have the loser of the first meeting as an underdog? If so, there could be value there. Use your Power Ranking tools to measure the value and invest if warranted.

Summary of Emotional Edges

We covered a lot of information in this section. Try not to retain all of it. Refer back to these pages as the year goes on. Though, it is important you do retain an overall feel for what our investing system entails.

This section again reinforces our overall NFL investment approach.

On the contrary to many popular handicapping beliefs, successful NFL investing involves *finding the emotional edges and gauging the sentiment of the betting public*. The scenarios outlined in this chapter continue to emphasis the main investment ideas.

The key takeaways from this section are:

- Uncovering an emotional edge is a power tool in finding investment value.

- Emotional Edges enable a less skillful team to play beyond their perceived ability

- The betting public (and oddsmakers) often overlook emotional edges (or lack of)

- NFL Investing Quarters – shift your overall investing mindset at different stages of the season

- Underdogs, especially home underdogs, can show you great investment value

- Teams can get complacent after blow out victories

- Primetime games have an enormous effect on a team's overall emotional state

- Scheduling analysis will allow you to realize emotional edges (or lack of)

- Divisional and non-divisional games can provide investment value

- 'Looking Ahead' is a receipt for an emotional letdown

Note – I realized schedule analysis can be difficult. So, I do offering all my in season alert 'Emotional Edge Alerts' through www.onlinewagerreview.com. We alert our premium members of upcoming scenarios that will show good betting value.

Visit our premium membership page at http://onlinewagerreview.com/nfl-rankings for more info.

NFL Statistical Analysis

Statistics with High Correlation to Win/Loss Record

As you have learned, our NFL investing approach is unlike many traditional handicapping systems.

We base our investments on properly gauging public sentiment, finding inaccurate lines and identifying emotional edges.

This approach "sentiment based approach" differs from the majority of system which handicap statistical matchups and scrimmage advantages.

But, statistics are not completely ignored in our investment approach.

How do we view statistics in our investing system?

Statistics are information, provided each week, in which we utilize to handicap each individual team and adjust our weekly power ranks.

With that said, we only focus *on statistics with high win/loss correlation.* In other words, statistics that have been determined to have a connection with the outcome of NFL games.

In this section, we will identify stats with high correlation to winning and review which statistics to focus on when adjusting your weekly Power Ranking.

In addition, we will highlight some useless stats that are often discussed, but have little or no bearing on the outcomes of football games.

Note - Stats will play a take a large role as more statistical information becomes available (later in the season). The reason is statistics will become more accurate as we get more occurrences (games played). Smoother statistical trends will begin to form and anomalies will be canceled out.

Yards per pass attempt (YDS/A)

Yards per pass attempt is by far the most important statistical category to focus on. Why? The NFL is a passing league - period. If a team cannot throw the ball effectively, they cannot move the football. If a team can't move the football, they cannot score points. If a team can't score points, the defense will be on the field the majority of the game. The trickledown effect of a poor passing game is enormous.

When YDS/A is calculated, it also takes into consideration incomplete passes and yards lost on sacks. Because these two dynamics are factored into this statistics, we can get a great feel of a team's overall offensive efficiency, at a glance.

When we review the top YDS/A leaders from 2011 (Table 8-A), we find the best teams in the league. Table 8-A clearly shows the high correlation between YDS/A and overall win/loss record.

Table 8-A: 2011 Yards Per Attempt (YDS/A) Leaders				
2011 Rank	Team	Yds/A	Record	Season Results
1	Green Bay	8.7	15-1	lost div playoffs
2	New England	8.3	13-3	lost Super Bowl
3	New Orleans	8.1	13-3	lost div playoffs
4	NY Giants	7.9	9-7	won Super Bowl

In a recent advanced NFL statistical study, YTD/A has been shown to have the highest correlation towards winning versus any other statistical measure[1]. The team that wins the pass per attempt battle will win the game over 75% of time. Again,

---

[1] Advancednflstats.com – What Makes a Team Win -
http://www.advancednflstats.com/2007/07/what-makes-teams-win-part-1.html

YDS/A is the most powerful statistic in our handicapping toolbox.

Yards Allowed per Pass Attempt (YDSa/A)

On the contrary to YDS/A, we analyze a team defensive efficiency by reviewing their Yards Allowed per Pass Attempt (YDSa/A).

For all the same reasons above, we can get an excellent feel of a team defensive unit by reviewing their YDSa/A numbers.

If a team is able to prevent a team from passing the ball effectively, this will show us that defensive unit is limiting opposing passing efficiency and spending less time on the field. A high ranking in YDSa/A defines a clear line of scrimmage advantage.

As you will see in Table 8-B, YDSa/A (like YDA/A) has high correlation to overall win/loss record. Historically, teams which rank well in Yards Allowed per Attempt have success winning football games.

Table 8-B: 2011 Yards Allowed Per Attempt Leaders				
2011 Rank	Team	Yds/A	Record	Season Results
1	Pittsburgh	5.6	12-4	lost in wildcard
2	Houston	5.6	10-6	lost in wildcard
3	Baltimore	5.9	12-4	lost div playoffs
4	Tennessee	6.1	9-7	no playoffs
5	San Francisco	6.3	13-3	lost NFL champ

'Big' or Explosive Plays

'Big Plays' are defined as a run or pass play that gains 20 yards or more. This statistic plays an enormous role in the modern NFL game. As you can imagine, it can be a tremendous advantage when a team is able to move the ball ⅕ the length of the field, in a single play.

Using Big Play totals, we are able to identify the big play offenses, at a glance. This allows us to recognize the teams who can rip off large chunks of yards. Clearly, large yardage chunks translate to points scored.

On the contrary, we use the "Big Plays" stat to identify defensive units who allow a larger amount of big plays per game. It can be demoralizing for defenses to allow big plays on a regular basis. As predicted, teams that are vulnerable to giving up large yardage chunks ultimately allow large point totals.

Table 8-C shows the best teams at limiting big plays during the 2009 NFL season. As you can see, the eventual Super Bowl winner (Indianapolis Colts) allowed the fewest big plays that year. The other top 3 teams had excellent success winning games.

Table 8-C - Plays allowed of 20-plus yards, 2009 Season				
Rank	Team	Big Plays	Record	Season Results
1	Colts	36	14-2	Won Super Bowl
2	Jets	41	9-7	lost in AFC title game
3	Chargers	43	13-3	lost in div round
4	Bengals	46	10-6	lost in wild card

Yard per Drive (YDS/Dr)

Yard per Drive is an excellent measure of a team's ability to move the football, on a consistent basis. If a team is able to move the ball then they put themselves in position to score points.
YDS/Dr is another simplified view of offensive efficiency, without confusing ourselves with useless statistics.

As you can see in Table 8-D, the best teams in the league rank at the top of Yards per Drive every season. As you can see, YDS/Dr is another statistic measure which possesses high correlation to overall win/loss record.

Table 8-D - 2011 YDS/Dr Leaders			
Rank	Team	Yds/Dr	Record
1	New Orleans	42.44	13-3
2	New England	39.53	13-3
3	Green Bay	39.43	15-1
4	San Diego	38.17	8-8
5	Pittsburg	35.58	12-4

Average Starting Field Position

Average starting field position is an important statistic when measuring a team defensive efficiency. This statistics is not a view of the kick return game. Rather, this statistic is a simple way of showing us which teams are playing good defense.

If a team ranks well in starting field position, it shows a team's defensive is limiting opponents to short drives and forcing opponents to punt from deep in their own zone. This is known as "hidden yardage" in the football game.

Use the guide below to determine where a team falls in the Average Starting Field Position category:

- Good Starting Field Position - 33 to 31 yard line
- Average Starting Field Position - 28 to 27 yard line
- Poor Starting Field Position - 25 to 23 yard line

In Table 8-E, you will find the 2011 leaders in average starting field position. Ranked on top of this list you will find the best defenses in the league.

Table 8-E - 2011 Avg Staring Field Position Leaders			
Rank	Team	Avg Starting Field Position	Defensive Rank
1	San Francisco	33.38	4
2	Seattle	31.21	9
3	Jets	30.86	5
4	Houston	30.36	2
5	Cincinnati	30.14	7

Statistics to Ignore

Many popular statistics highlighted by the NFL media are meaningless and should be completely ignored. These statistics sound good when used in a television or radio broadcast, but ultimately have little correlation to outcomes of football games.

Let's look at some examples and discuss why they are misleading.

Total Yards or Total Yards Allowed

The total yardarge statistics are the most misconceived stats analyzed in the modern NFL game.

As we will show you, total yards stats have little or no bearing on an outcome of football games. Reason being, they can be easily skewed if one team is dominating the game.

Here is an example - If a team is winning the game by a large margin they will shift into prevent defense. This will loosen up pass coverage and allow big holes to run through. But there is strategy involved. The team leading is only looking for the opposing team to keep the clock running and 'shorten the game'. The yardage gained in this part of the game is known as 'garbage yardage'. Garbage yardage is defines as yardage gained when the outcome of the game has already been determined.

You will often hear the media label a defense as 'bends but doesn't break'. The reality is, that football team is more than likely dominating football games, but allowing big yard late or garbage yardage, while protecting a lead.

For evidence of this, see the Table 8-F. Here we have listed the worst total yardage allowed per game ranks for the 2011 season.

Table 8-F - 2011 Worst Total Yardage per Game Allowed			
Rank	Team	Yds Allowed/game	2011 Record
32	Green Bay	411.6	15-1
31	New England	411.1	13-3

As you can see, in respects to total yardage allowed per game, Green Bay and New England were ranked last and second to last.

Did these total yardage statistics have any correlation to their overall record? Zero.

In 2011, the two worst yardage allowed teams in the league held a combined 28 and 4 record! Green Bay nearly went undefeated.

This should be enough evidence to never again put one thought into total yardage numbers when investing in NFL football.

Total Rushing Attempts

We have all heard a stat like this before - "When this team rushes the ball 25 times they are 5-0 blah blah blah." This is misleading. The reality is, total rushing attempts have little correlation to the outcomes of football games.

To prove this point, let's review the rushing statistics from 2011 season. In Table 8-G, we have listed the highest rushing attempts per game versus overall record.

Table 8-G - 2011 Most Rushing Attempts per Game			
Rank	Team	Att/G	Record
1	San Francisco	34.1	8-8
2	Seattle	34.1	10-6
3	Jets	31.1	13-3
4	Houston	30.6	5-11
5	Cincinnati	30.4	7-9
6	Miami Dolphins	29.3	6-10

Do you see any positive correlation between rushing attempts and record? Nope. Do any positive patterns exist between a team running the ball in volume and them winning games? None. There is no positive correlation between rushing attempts and a team winning a football game.

Totally disregard any rush attempt statistics you see going forward. The fact is, a team will rack up rushing attempts after establishing a solid lead. Running the ball late will protect the ball and run out the clock. This is the main function of the run game in modern day football.

Summary of Statistical Analysis

In summary, do not be confused by football statistics. Unfortunately, most stats tossed around by the modern media are just noise and should be ignored.

Simply, use the statistics (outlined above) which show high correlation to overall win/loss record. Apply these statistics you your overall league and team opinions. Then, make the necessary adjustments to your weekly power ranking.

Some of the stats previously highlighted are not easily found. So, we have listed several websites in our appendix section where you can find these stats online.

Statistics with High Correlation to Win/Loss Record:

- Yards Per Pass Attempt (YDS/A)
- Yards Allowed Per Pass Attempt (YDSa/A)
- Big or Explosive Plays
- Yards Per Drive (YDS/Dr)
- Average Starting Field Position

Statistics to Ignore:

- Total Yardage
- Total Yardage Allowed
- Rushing Attempts per Game

More on Profitable NFL Investing

NFL Media, Betting Work Week and Money Management

In this section, we will highlight a few additional NFL investing tips that will help you wager successfully on NFL football.

First, we will look at how evaluate the NFL media and how to use them when planning your wagers.

Then, we will also show you how to plan your betting week. We will review the workweek of a top NFL investor.

Finally, we will review money management. We will discuss proper wagering amount, long term goals and how to manage your money correctly throughout the NFL season.

NFL Sports Media - How to use them to your advantage

The NFL sports media can be a powerful ally in your search for NFL betting value. As you have read, our entire NFL strategy is based on finding inaccurate point spreads (lines).

So, how does the NFL media help us do this?

Simple - we bet against them.

Here's an example, let's say the New England Patriots are on a roll. They have been blowing out opponents the last few weeks (35+ points maybe?). Suddenly, the Patriots provide the hot story for the NFL media. During the week, ESPN will be highlighting the Patriots. They breaking down every play, talking of Super Bowl and having every 'expert' weigh in with their opinion.

What does this overexposure do to the betting public? You guessed it - the sentiment towards the Patriots becomes one side. The betting public will be saturated with Patriot overcoverage and be looking to place money on the Patriots (to cover) in their upcoming games.

Don't be fooled. The oddsmakers are watching this very closely, too. When they set the next New England point spread they will be sure to overcompensate for public sentiment shift and overexposure. They will set the Patriots as a bigger favorite then they should be - this is called 'juicing the line' or 'added chalk'. This leads to an inaccurate line by oddsmakers, hence creating investment value.

Furthermore, the rest of the league is taking notice. NFL players watch ESPN too. They take note of media ranting and raving about the Patriots. The preverbal 'target on the back' has been set. Upcoming opponent of the Patriots will be extra charged to face the 'media darlings'. Teams will take pride in possibly defeating the seemingly invincible Patriots. This will lead to a week of spirited practices and extra preparation for their upcoming challenge.

In summarizing this example, excess media coverage has caused an inaccurate line and emotional edge for the opposing team. Throw it all together and you have a powerful receipt of intangibles that no statistic can quantify. These are they investment opportunities we will capitalize on.

Note – nothing can exemplify our theories of NFL wagering better than the example above. By this point it should be clear that these are the types of intangibles you will profit from in your future NFL wagering ventures.

Throughout the season, be observant of media coverage that will shift the sentiment of the betting public. When you identify this shift, look to bet against the team getting over-covered by the NFL media. The chances are high you will be getting excellent value on your underdog lines.

Additional Notes on the NFL Media:

- Go against the masses - Always look to go against the masses and the sentiment of the public. Use the media to gauge this sentiment.

- Statistics - Don't listen to the stats the media throws out. For the most part, they are meaningless. They just sound good to the novice fan.

- Do not follow "expert picks" - Most TV personalities covering NFL football are far from experts, especially when it comes to picking winners.

- Do your own homework - as we will cover later, it important to do your own homework when reviewing an NFL matchup. The highlights on ESPN and NFL Network only give you a small piece of the true story.

The Guide to NFL Investing

How to Plan Your Betting Week

In this section, we will show you to plan your NFL investing week. Like a top Wall Street money manager, we will be approaching our workweek with discipline and passion. Serious NFL investing takes time and effort.

Note – we understand that not everyone can dedicate the same amount of time toward their NFL wagering. If your time is limited, use the following information as a general guide, and adjust the plan according to what works best for you.

Sunday - Game Day

The best day week! This is the day we watch all the NFL action unfold. But, what is the best way to watch the games? And how to we plan out our Sundays?

Watching the Games - Try to concentrate closely on 4 or 5 games. Attempt to get a real feel for the action. How did a team react to a tough situation? How did the team respond when down 4 points late in the game? How did they protect their quarterback? Taking notes (sometimes mental) along the way and trying to absorb the details of the games.

Note - We love the Red Zone Network, but this can sometimes give you an inaccurate perception of a game. Try to watch the complete game on NFL Sunday Ticket.

Highlights and Review - At around 7 or 8PM EST Sunday night, we review all the day's action. We visit NFL.com or tune into NFL Network to review the highlights of the day. We also review the box scores online. Again, we try to get a real feel for the ebbs and flows of the day's games.

Sunday Night Game - As for the Sunday Night game, we would have more than likely handicapped this game earlier in the week. So, be sure not to just wager on this game just for the sake of betting. We will watch the Sunday night game, focusing primarily on how this game will affect the upcoming games for the teams involved (see emotional edges in Part 7).

Adjust Power Rankings - As we are watching the Sunday Night game, we will review all the box scores from the day's games to get real story of each game. We will note the day's action and make any adjustments to our power rankings at this time.

Play Odds Maker - After we make our adjustments to our power rankings, we will play oddsmaker. We will review the next week matchups and apply our Power Rankings/Point spread cheat sheet (Table 7-3) to set our line.

Check out the Early Lines - After playing oddsmaker and setting our proprietary lines, we will check out the offshore sportsbooks early lines (Many top online sportsbooks will offer lines early lines). You will notice some of our power ranking lines may be very similar to the sportsbook lines. But, if we see a significant difference between our line and the early sportsbook lines – we may discover investing value for the next week. This is how we identify possible bets.

Monday - Investments coming into focus

When Monday arrives, we will have a good idea of how our next week's wagering is shaping up. We may place bets early Monday morning if we feel the line has good value and it may move against us (or value may disappear). If we feel the line will move in our favor (as the week goes on) then we will hold off betting that game until later in the week.

Watch the NFL Media - Monday is a good day to get a feel for the teams who are gaining media coverage. The NFL 'experts' will start to express their opinions on which the best teams are. Take notice of the teams getting overexposure which can cause a public sentiment shift in their favor. As we mentioned, we will look to go against this popular sentiment.

Place Bets/Line Movers - We will also check the Vegas and Offshore sportsbooks for any significant line movement. This will give us another indication where the early money is going. We will now place our bets on any games we have previously found value in and we feel the value will disappear.

Monday Night Game - We have done our homework on the Monday Night game earlier in the week. So again, resist the temptation to wager on the Monday Night game just for the 'action'. We will watch the Monday Night game paying close attention to the details of the game. As with the Sunday Night game, our primary focus will be on how the outcome of this game could affect upcoming games (and emotional scenarios).

Remember - we pay close attention to the outcomes of the Sunday and Monday Night games. Often these games give the betting public an inaccurate view of the teams due to the overexposure of a primetime game. Additionally, the outcome of the game can have a large effect on the emotional states of both the winning and losing team (as discussed in Part 7).

After the Monday Night game, we adjust our power rankings for the two teams involved.

Tuesday - Monday Night Teams, Injuries

On Tuesday, we will again review the sportsbook lines, especially taking notice of the upcoming lines for the teams who played Monday night. At this time, we will often place our wagers involving a Monday Night team (since these lines have a great chance to be set inaccurately).

Injuries - On this day we will also review any player injuries. These injury reports will be preliminary, but we can get a good feel for any substantial injuries that may affect our power rankings.

Wednesday through Saturday - Keep in Tune

During the rest of the week, we will keep in tune with the point spreads we are looking to invest in. We will continue to check the lines and note any significant moves for games in which we have interest. If a line reaches a point where we think value has been maximized, we will place our wager.

Note on Point Spreads - when checking lines during the week, check several top online NFL sportsbooks to see who offers the best lines (also known as "shopping lines"). Since we have accounts at multiple sportsbooks, we are able to compare the lines/value and wager at the book that offers the best line for our wager. These line comparisons are an important part of money management that will be discussed in the next section.

Injuries - We will also keep in tune will all the official injury reports released by the teams. These reports are helpful, but to determine if an injured player will suit up you must watch the practice report. Pay close attention to the Friday practices. If a player misses the Friday practice (walk-through) - he will more than likely not play in that week's game.

Sunday - Pre-Game Line Movement

Lines do not move much between Wednesday and Saturday. But, Sunday morning you may see some heavy one-side betting move a line.

We view this late betting action as the novice public money, with no real substance behind their wagers. Occasionally, this late action will push a line enough so we will bet the other side (against the betting public). We will only bet these late Sunday line moves if the line shows value in our power ranking tools.

Recap and Summary of Planning Your Betting Week

Like Wall Street investing, successful NFL handicapping takes a lot of work. All successful NFL handicappers have a similar work ethic as we outlined above. We don't just roll out of bed Sunday morning and place our wagers. A continued study of the league and the betting sentiment is needed to gain an investing edge.

Sunday:

1. Watch the details of the games

2. Review box scores and highlights

3. Adjust Power Rankings

4. Play Oddsmaker, set your lines using power rankings

5. Compare your lines to the early sportsbook lines

6. Watch Sunday Night Game, How will this effect next week's action?

Monday:

1. Place your bets on games that show value that may disappear

2. Watch the media, what team is getting overexposure?

3. Monday Night Game - How will this effect next week's action?

4. Adjust your power rankings for teams in the Monday Night game

Tuesday:

1. Check Lines of Monday Night teams

2. Place wager on teams involved in the previous Monday Night game

3. Watch for early injury reports that can effect power rankings

Wednesday - Saturday:

1. Keep in tune with the lines of the games you want to bet

2. Watch practice and injury reports

Sunday Morning:

1. Watch late public betting action

2. Bet against the public if Power Rankings show value

Money Management - Long Term Perspective

As you have learned, we view NFL wagering as an investment.

When investing, you will not win 100% of the time. Like every successful real estate investor or stock speculator, NFL handicappers do not get discouraged by short term losses. They have a clear understanding of the big picture.

So, what are the long term goals of an NFL handicapper?

Over the long-term - A good NFL handicapper will win between 55-60% of his bets. During the short term - any results are possible.

Before you can seriously wager on NFL games you should have this 'win rate' goal in mind. To have the correct mindset, it's vital to be realistic with your goals. This target win percentage of 55-60% is an excellent profitability goal that will give you long term profits from your NFL investments.

When picking NFL football at a 55% win rate, you will have an edge of 3% over the sportsbooks. At first glance, this 3% edge may seem small, but it's a tremendous advantage to have in gambling. For a comparison, in the game of blackjack, a player only needs a 1% edge to be profitable long-term.

Let's use these win percentages in real dollar amounts to show how this 'win rate' effects profitability and return on investment.

For this example, we will place 100 NFL wagers (about 1 season worth of wagers). On each wager, we risk $110 to profit $100 (remember - the majority of NFL wagers are placed at 11 to 10 odds, or -110). In the Table 8-A, we show the net profits difference, using different win rate percentages.

Table 8-A - Win Rate, Profitability and Return on Investment						
Win Rate	50%	53%	55%	57%	60%	62%
Wagers Won	50	53	55	57	60	62
Wagers Lost	50	47	45	43	40	38
Money Won	5000	5300	5500	5700	6000	6200
Money Lost	5500	5170	4950	4730	4400	4180
Net Profit	-$500	$130	$550	$970	$1,600	$2,020
Return on Investment (ROI)	-4.5%	1.2%	5.0%	8.8%	14.5%	18.4%
Annualized ROI	-11%	3%	12%	22%	39%	50%
Total Wagers	100	100	100	100	100	100
Total Wagered	$11,000	$11,000	$11,000	$11,000	$11,000	$11,000

Note – in this example we are using consistent wager amounts. Adjusting wagering amounts will allow you to increase profits. We will discuss wager amounts later in this section.

As you can see, an NFL bettor needs to win approximately 53% (or 53 bets out of 100) to profit from the 11-10 odds of NFL investing.

Furthermore, if a handicapper picks at 60% (which is very obtainable) they realize a return of +15% in a five month span, which equates to a 50% annualized return on investment! This a better return than you'll get in a savings account, a money market or the stock market over the last 10 years.

Remember, any outcome is possible in the short term. Even the most talented handicappers will have losing streaks. Ultimately, losses are inevitable. There will be times when your rankings are off or you just have the wrong feeling towards a team. Just remember, just as in Wall Street, *successful NFL investors never lose sight of long term goals.*

Wager Amounts

What is the correct way to plan your wager amounts? We have taken this approach from over 10 years of stock speculation and applied a similar technique to our betting system.

It's a very simple money management technique will allow you to maximize winners and weather losing streaks during the season.

For our investment amounts, we set the standard amount at 2.5% of our bankroll. Games we feel strongly about or bigger bets - we up our wager to 3.5% of our total bankroll. For games that we are less confident about - we gear back to 2% of your bankroll.

For example, let's say your bankroll is $10,000 to start the NFL season. We recommend a standard wager amount of $250. Bigger bets would be in $350 range and a small bet $200.

As your bankroll fluctuates during the season, you make adjustments accordingly. If your bankroll grows to $15,000 - a standard bet would grow to $375 (2.5% of $15,000), a large bet moves to $525 (3.5% of $15,000) and so on.

This would be viewed as a conservative approach to money management. Feel free to adjust your wager amounts according to your risk tolerance. But remember - it's most important to keep the long term perspective in focus and not go broke before these trends take effect.

Just as in stock speculation, money management holds top importance. You could have the best betting or investment system in the world - but if you broke – you will have no money to invest in it.

Final Thoughts

In this guide we have outlined a very powerful football investment system. Learning this NFL investment approach was your first step to successfully wagering on NFL football.

Remember, NFL investing is not about stats or player matchups.

Successfully betting NFL football is about gauging the public betting sentiment and finding inaccurate lines set off these inaccurate views of the league.

As they say on Wall Street – he who is in touch with the sentiment of the market, wins.

The same holds true in NFL wagering and investing.

Now you have the knowledge to properly invest in NFL football like a Wall Street professional.

Sincerely,

PS – I will be posting my proprietary weekly rankings and investment picks to premium users on OnlineWagerReview.com.

Feel free to visit us at www.onlinewagerreview.com/nfl-rankings for more info.

Appendix

Power Rankings/Margin of Victory Cheat Sheet

Table 7-3
Power Rankings/Point Spread Cheat Sheet

Away Team		Home Team										
		A	B+	B	B-	C+	C	C-	D+	D	D-	F
	A	-2.5	0.5	2.5	4	5	8	11	14	15.5	17	21
	B+	-5.5	-2.5	-0.5	1	2	5	8	11	12.5	14	18
	B	-7.5	-4.5	-2.5	-1	0	3	6	9	10.5	12	16
	B-	-9	-6	-4	-2.5	-1.5	1.5	4.5	7.5	9	10.5	14.5
	C+	-10	-7	-5	-3.5	-2.5	0.5	3.5	6.5	8	9.5	13.5
	C	-13	-10	-8	-6.5	-5.5	-2.5	0.5	3.5	5	6.5	10.5
	C-	-16	-13	-11	-9.5	-8.5	-5.5	-2.5	0.5	2	3.5	7.5
	D+	-19	-16	-14	-12.5	-11.5	-8.5	-5.5	-2.5	-1	0.5	4.5
	D	-20.5	-17.5	-15.5	-14	-13	-10	-7	-4	-2.5	-1	3
	D-	-22	-19	-17	-15.5	-14.5	-11.5	-8.5	-5.5	-4	-2.5	1.5
	F	-26	-23	-21	-19.5	-18.5	-15.5	-12.5	-9.5	-8	-6.5	-2.5

Power Ranking Grade, Overall Record

Table 7-1 Overall Record Power Rankings		
Grade	Overall Wins	Overall Losses
A	16	0
A	15	1
A	14	2
A	13	3
B+	12	4
B	11	5
B-	10	6
C+	9	7
C	8	8
C-	7	9
C-	6	10
D+	5	11
D	4	12
D-	3	13
F	2	14
F	1	15
F	0	16

Power Rankings, Margin of Victory, Total Wins

Table 7-2		
Correlation Between Margin of Victory and Overall Record		
Ranking	Average Margin of Victory	Total Wins
A	10.5	13 to 16
B+	7.5	12
B	5.5	11
B-	4	10
C+	3	9
C	0	8
C-	-3	7,6
D+	-6	5
D	-7.5	4
D-	-9	3
F	-13	2 to 0

Definitions:

Big (explosive) Play: a run or pass play that gains 20 yards or more

Big Game: a game against a divisional rival or versus a top 5 team in the league

Caught Looking Ahead: When a team is looking past their current opponent and experience a letdown

Divisional Sandwich Game - a team plays a divisional game, then a non-division (or non-conference) game, then a divisional game the third week

Emotional Edge: An intangible force that causes a football team to have added motivation for an upcoming game or opponent. Possibly playing beyond their perceived skill level

False Favorites: When a team is incorrectly set as a favorite by oddsmakers.

Favorite Bias: the betting public's stronger sentiment to bet favorites

Garbage Yardage: Yardage gained when the outcome of the game has already been determined

Juice – fee charged by sportsbooks for accepting your bet. For football betting usually set at 10% of wager amount

Juicing the Line or Extra Chalk: when bookmakers add additional points to a favorite in the hopes to balance the one-sided betting activity

Media Darlings - who the media is overhyping at any given time

Point Spread – the handicap, in terms of points, by which a stronger team is expected to defeat a weaker one

Sell Short - bet against a team

Shorten the game: when leading the game, allow the other team to move the football in the hopes to keeping the clock running

Underdog Motivation: Added motivation a team encounters when they know they are the perceived less skillful team

Vigorish (or Vig): also known as juice, the fee charged by sportsbooks for accepting your bet. For football betting usually set at 10% of wager amount

NFL Statistical References:

USA Today: *Game Box Scores:*

http://content.usatoday.com/sportsdata/scores/nfl

NFL.com: *Team Statistics (Big Plays of 20+ yards)*

http://www.nfl.com/stats/team

Teamrankings.com: *Passing Yards Per Attempt (YDS/A)*

http://www.teamrankings.com/nfl/stat/yards-per-pass-attempt

Passing Yards Allowed Per Attempt (YDSA/A)

http://www.teamrankings.com/nfl/stat/opponent-yards-per-pass-attempt

FootballOutsiders.com: *Average Starting Field Position & Yards Per Drive*

http://www.footballoutsiders.com/stats/drivestats

AdvancedNFLStats.com: *Highest Correlation between Stats and Wins*

http://www.advancednflstats.com/2007/07/what-makes-teams-win-part-1.html

NFL Margin of Victory Study – Raw Data

Total Wins vs. Average Margin of Victory (2001 to 2011):

Wins	Average Margin Victory
16	19.69
15	10.06
14	10.82
13	9.57
12	7.35
11	5.38
10	3.80
9	2.55
8	-0.22
7	-2.64
6	-2.51
5	-6.00
4	-7.64
3	-8.89
2	-11.85
1	-12.25
0	-15.56

How the NFL Schedule is Created

Currently, each team's 16-game regular season schedule is set using a pre-determined formula:*

- Each team plays the other three teams in their division twice: once at home, and once on the road (six games).

- Each team plays the four teams from another division within its own conference once on a rotating three-year cycle: two at home, and two on the road (four games).

- Each team plays the four teams from a division in the other conference once on a rotating four-year cycle: two at home, and two on the road (four games).

- Each team plays once against the other teams in its conference that finished in the same place in their own divisions as themselves in the previous season, not counting the division they were already scheduled to play: one at home, one on the road (two games).

*Source - 2012 Opponents Determined". NFL. January 2, 2012. Retrieved January 23, 2012.

http://nfllabor.files.wordpress.com/2012/01/2012-opponents-determined.pdf

Made in the USA
Middletown, DE
27 January 2017